THE POISONOUS MUSHROOM

CLEMENS & BLAIR, LLC

Other titles from the publisher include:

Mein Kampf, by Adolf Hitler (New English Translation)
The Essential Mein Kampf, by Adolf Hitler
On the Jews and Their Lies, by Martin Luther
Passovers of Blood, by Ariel Toaff

Other books written or edited by Thomas Dalton include:

Debating the Holocaust (4th ed.)
The Holocaust: An Introduction
Goebbels on the Jews
The Jewish Hand in the World Wars
Hitler on the Jews
Eternal Strangers: Critical Views of Jews and Judaism
Streicher, Rosenberg, and the Jews: The Nuremberg Transcripts

For details, see www.thomasdaltonphd.com

The Poisonous Mushroom

Ernst Hiemer

Translated from the German
"DER GIFTPILZ"
Originally published in 1938

New York, London
CLEMENS & BLAIR, LLC

CLEMENS & BLAIR, LLC

Original German text: 1938

This edition, edited and copyright © 2020, by Thomas Dalton, PhD

All rights reserved. No part of this publication may be reproduced, stored in a retrieval system, or transmitted, in any form or by any means, electronic, mechanical, photocopying, recording, or otherwise.

Clemens & Blair, LLC, is a non-profit educational publisher.

Library of Congress Cataloging-in-Publication Data

Hiemer, Ernst (1900-1974)

The Poisonous Mushroom (*Der Giftpilz*)

       p.   cm.

Includes bibliographical references.

ISBN 978-1734-8042-25 (pbk.: alk. paper)

1. Religion. 2. Judaism.

Printing number: 9 8 7 6 5 4 3 2 1

Printed in the United States of America on acid-free paper.

Foreword and Disclaimer, by Thomas Dalton, PhD	9
Chapter 1: THE POISONOUS MUSHROOM	19
Chapter 2: HOW TO IDENTIFY A JEW	23
Chapter 3: HOW THE JEWS CAME TO US	25
Chapter 4: WHAT IS THE TALMUD?	29
Chapter 5: WHY THE JEWS LET THEMSELVES BE BAPTIZED	35
Chapter 6: HOW A GERMAN PEASANT WAS DRIVEN FROM HOUSE AND FARM	37
Chapter 7: HOW JEWISH TRADERS CHEAT	39
Chapter 8: THE EXPERIENCE OF HANS AND ELSE WITH A STRANGE MAN	43
Chapter 9: INGE'S VISIT TO A JEWISH DOCTOR	45
Chapter 10: HOW THE JEW TREATS HIS DOMESTIC HELP	51
Chapter 11: HOW TWO WOMEN WERE TRICKED BY JEWISH LAWYERS	53
Chapter 12: HOW JEWS TORMENT ANIMALS	57
Chapter 13: WHAT JESUS SAID ABOUT THE JEWS	59
Chapter 14: MONEY IS THE GOD OF THE JEWS	63
Chapter 15: HOW MR. HARTMANN BECAME A NATIONAL SOCIALIST	65
Chapter 16: ARE THERE DECENT JEWS?	69
Chapter 17: NO SALVATION WITHOUT SOLVING THE JEWISH QUESTION	71

THE POISONOUS MUSHROOM

FOREWORD AND DISCLAIMER
THOMAS DALTON, PHD

The following children's book was written during Nazi Germany's height of power, in 1938. Hitler's government had overcome the corruption and decay of the Weimar Regime that had ruled Germany after World War One, and, amidst a global depression that was destroying the lives of millions in the West, succeeded in raising up a crippled and defeated nation to become a world power. As with all successful nations, its leaders sought to promote their values and their worldview among the public, and especially among the youth. Hence it is not surprising that someone should have undertaken to write a children's book condemning the primary domestic enemy of the German people: the Jews.

Hitler, of course, had long attacked the Jews as enemies of the German nation. And not without good reason. To his east was the communist Soviet Union—a nation created by Jews (Lenin and Trotsky), founded on the Jewish-Marxist ideology known as Bolshevism, and run, for many years, by Jews. Upon coming to power in 1918, Bolshevik Jews proceeded to launch a brutal civil war that led to the deaths of at least 20 million Russians, and perhaps many more. The rest of that nation was enslaved in a crushing Soviet system that scarcely needs describing. By the 1930s, this very Soviet Bolshevism was growing in power, and threatening to invade central Europe. To Hitler's west, in England and the USA, were the capitalist Jews who hated him and the Nazi party that had overthrown the Weimar Jews; these capitalists badly wanted to crush the German nation economically, if not militarily. And then thirdly, internally, were the 500,000 German Jews who also hated Hitler and the very German people who elected him to power. Therefore, Hitler was threatened by Jews left, right, and center.

Thus, it is unsurprising that Hitler and others of the Nazi leadership would speak of Jews in the harshest of terms: as enemies of the people, as destroyers of nations, as a disease, as a threat to morality and common decency. And indeed, Hitler was not alone; German philosophers and scholars had, for many years, spoken out on the deleterious effect of Jews on the German people. And before that, for centuries, perceptive scholars of many nations and ages had condemned the Jews as a dangerous and malignant people, as crude materialists, as deceptive and immoral liars, as hateful misanthropes, and as parasites on other nations. Hitler was only the latest in a long line—stretching over 2,000 years—of men who detested the Jews, and who sought to free their people from the malicious Jewish influence.[1]

One of Hitler's earliest comrades was Julius Streicher—a school teacher and political organizer from Nuremberg. Though never a ranking member of the Nazi government, Streicher eventually became the local district leader in Nuremberg, all while producing and disseminating pro-Nazi, anti-Jewish literature. His primary means was the small newspaper *Der Stürmer*, which he published from 1923 until the end of the war. Among his co-workers there was a man named Ernst Hiemer—also a school teacher, and also strongly committed to the Nazi program. In addition to serving as chief editor of *Der Stürmer*, Hiemer wrote books for children that featured anti-Semitic themes and morals. The first and most notorious of these was *Der Giftpilz*—"The Poisonous Mushroom." The book featured notable sketches and artwork by a prominent cartoonist, Philipp Rupprecht. The full text and artwork are reproduced here.

---

[1] For details, see the book *Eternal Strangers*, by T. Dalton (2020).

THE POISONOUS MUSHROOM

«《—》»

The German title of the book, *Der Giftpilz*, is a straightforward compound word: *gift* (poison) + *pilz* (mushroom). The metaphor here was likely drawn from Hitler's terminology, especially in his primary work *Mein Kampf*. There, Hitler repeatedly referred to the "poisonous" nature of the Jews; he makes mention of "this poison" (*dieses Gift*) of global Jewry, of their "poisoning the soul" (*die Seelen vergiften*) of the German people, of the Jews' "poisonous clutches" (*giftigen Seuche*), of "Jewish poisoners of the people" (*jüdischen Volksvergifter*), and of Jewish attempts to destroy a nation's racial purity through "a continuous poisoning of the individual" (*dauernde Vergiftung der einzelnen*).[2] Later in the book he refers to the Jews as an "international world-poison" (*internationalen Weltvergiftung*).[3] The 'mushroom' metaphor occurs only once; in Volume One, Hitler refers to the Jews as the "eternal fungus" (*ewiger Spaltpilz*) of humanity[4]—though there is a double-entendre here, in that the word Spaltpilz also colloquially refers to a disruptive force in society.

The text of this book is of course aimed at children, roughly those aged 8 to 14, though with messages for older teens and even parents. Each of the 17 small chapters consists of a short vignette or morality play intended to show the dangers of Jews in German society. Some are purely fictional, but most have some basis in fact, and are drawn from actual events in history. Many Jews indeed have a characteristic look, such as a big nose, bushy eyebrows, or being short (chapter 2)—though today, plastic surgery hides many of these features. Jews indeed adopt local languages and names (chapter 3) while still retaining an essentially Jewish mindset. The Talmud (chapter 4) does in fact have many anti-Gentile

---

[2] See *Mein Kampf*, volume one, sections 2.23, 5.7, and 11.20.
[3] Volume two, section 6.2
[4] Section 3.29.

passages, many of which are drawn from the Old Testament.[5] To hide their presence, Jews often did 'convert' to Christianity (chapter 5), though without giving up their true beliefs. Jewish bankers did indeed frequently make loans to farmers at exceptionally high interest rates (usury), and if the farmer could not pay, they were quick to seize his land (chapter 6).

Later chapters refer, for example, to Jesus' view of the Jews (chapter 13). Jesus did indeed call them "a brood of vipers" (Matt 3:7, 12:34, 23:33), and the Jews did say "Let him be crucified" (Matt 27:22). Luke (15:14) calls the Jews "lovers of money". In John (8:44), Jesus says "You [Jews] are of your father, the devil" who was a "murderer" and "the father of lies." In his text, Hiemer simply takes such messages and casts them in the form of compact moral stories.

Upon its release in 1938, the book sold well, running to a circulation of around 60,000. We should note that this was well before the "Holocaust" allegedly began (in late 1941), and even before such incidents as *Kristallnacht* (November 1938). There was no question, at that time, of physically harming Jews; Hiemer and Streicher simply wanted to warn the people, and especially children, of long-standing hazards of dealing with Jews. The book ends with a reference to the urgency of some kind of "solution" to the Jewish Question, but the nature of that solution is left entirely open. From Streicher's other writings, we know that he had advocated deporting German Jews to some location outside of Europe, such as the island of Madagascar, but this notion did not find its way into *The Poisonous Mushroom*.

---

[5] In Deuteronomy (15:6), Moses tells the Jews "you shall rule over many nations"; "they shall be afraid of you" (28:10). We can cite Genesis: "Let peoples serve you, and nations bow down to you" (27:29); or Deuteronomy, where God promises Jews "houses full of all good things, which [they] did not fill, and cisterns hewn out, which [they] did not hew, and vineyards and olive trees, which [they] did not plant" (6:11). And we can read in Isaiah: "Foreigners shall build up your walls, and their kings shall minister to you…that men may bring you the wealth of the nations" (60:10-11); or again, "aliens shall stand and feed your flocks, foreigners shall be your plowmen and vinedressers…you shall eat the wealth of the nations" (61:5-6). Here we see explicit contempt for Gentiles.

THE POISONOUS MUSHROOM

««—»»

Eventually, of course, war did come to Germany and to all the world, and indeed there was a prominent Jewish hand in that war.[6] Germany would ultimately lose, as we know, and Hitler would perish at his own hand. Globally, some 60 million people would die.

Both Hiemer and Rupprecht, however, would survive the war. Rupprecht was captured, sentenced to hard labor, and released in 1950. He died in Munich in 1975. Hiemer spent nearly four years at Stalag 13, was released, and died in 1974. For his part, Streicher also survived the wars years; but just barely. He was captured and put on trial as a "major Nazi war criminal" during the Nuremberg trials. He was found guilty, sentenced to death, and hanged in October 1946.[7]

The Poisonous Mushroom remains, to this day, a fascinating remnant of the Nazi era, and as explicit documentation of the beliefs and ideals of at least some members of the National Socialist system. Such a book is unimaginable today, but at the time it did serve an important purpose for German society. It was a true reflection of the times.

DISCLAIMER: Neither the publisher nor the editor endorses the ideas in the present work. It is presented here strictly as a work of historical interest, nothing more. Any resemblances to actual Jews, living or dead, are purely coincidental.

---

[6] See the book *The Jewish Hand in the World Wars*, by T. Dalton (2019).
[7] For an interesting account of Streicher's role at Nuremberg, and his personal testimony, see *Streicher, Rosenberg, and the Jews*, by T. Dalton (2020).

The Poisonous Mushroom

THE POISONOUS MUSHROOM

Just as it is often hard to tell a poisonous toadstool from an edible mushroom, so too it is often very hard to recognize the Jew as a swindler and criminal.

CHAPTER ONE

The Poisonous Mushroom

A mother and her young son are gathering mushrooms in the German forest. The boy finds some poisonous ones. The mother explains that there are good mushrooms and there are poisonous ones; as they go home, she says:

"Look, Franz, human beings in this world are like the mushrooms in the forest. There are good mushrooms and there are good people. There are poisonous, bad mushrooms and there are bad people. And we have to be on our guard against bad people, just as we have against poisonous mushrooms. Do you understand that?"

"Yes, mother," Franz replies. "I understand that in dealing with bad people, trouble may arise, just as when one eats a poisonous mushroom. One may even die!"

"And do you know, too, who these bad men are, these poisonous mushrooms of mankind?" mother continued.

Franz slaps his chest in pride: "Of course I know, mother! They are the Jews! Our teacher has often told us about them."

THE POISONOUS MUSHROOM

The mother praises her son for his intelligence, and goes on to explain the different kinds of poisonous Jews: the Jewish peddler, the Jewish cattle dealer, the Kosher butcher, the Jewish doctor, the baptized Jew, and so on.

"However they disguise themselves, or however friendly they try to be, affirming a thousand times their good intentions to us, one must not believe them. Jews they are, and Jews they remain. For our people, they are poison."

"Like the poisonous mushroom!" says Franz.

"Yes, my child! Just as a single poisonous mushroom can kill a whole family, so a solitary Jew can destroy a whole village, a whole city, even an entire people."

Franz has understood. "Tell me, mother, do all non-Jews know that the Jew is as dangerous as a poisonous mushroom?"

Mother shakes her head. "Unfortunately not, my child. There are millions of non-Jews who do not yet know the Jews. So we have to enlighten people and warn them against the Jews. Our young people, too, must be warned. Our boys and girls must learn to know the Jew. They must learn that the Jew is the most dangerous poison mushroom in existence. Just as poisonous mushrooms spring up everywhere, so the Jew is found in every country in the world. Just as poisonous mushrooms often lead to the most dreadful calamity, so the Jew is the cause of misery and distress, illness and death."

THE POISONOUS MUSHROOM

German youth must learn to recognize the Jewish poison mushroom. They must learn what a danger the Jew is for the German people and for the whole world. They must learn that the Jewish problem involves the destiny of us all.

The following tales tell the truth about the Jewish poison mushroom. They show the many shapes the Jew assumes. They show the depravity and baseness of the Jewish race. They show the Jew for what he really is:

The Devil in human form.

THE POISONOUS MUSHROOM

The Jewish nose is bent. It looks like the number six.

CHAPTER TWO

How to Identify a Jew

The boys' class is dealing with the question of how to recognize a Jew. Their teacher, Mr. Birkmann, has made various drawings on the blackboard to assist the class. A boy, Karl, stands in front of the board with a pointer and explains the drawings:

"One can tell a Jew by his nose. The Jewish nose is bent at the tip. It looks like a figure 6. So we call them 'Figure Sixes.' Many non-Jews also have bent noses. But in their case, the nose is bent up, not down. They have nothing to do with the Jewish nose."

Encouraged by the teacher, Karl points out that the lips are another distinguishing feature; they are usually puffed up. The eyebrows are usually thicker and fuller than ours.

From the eyes, one can see that the Jew is: A false, deceitful person.

The best student in the class, Fritz Mueller, then comes to the front and continues. Fritz points out that Jews are usually middle-sized and have short legs. Their arms too, are usually short. Many Jews have curved legs and are flat-footed. They often have a low slanting forehead. We call it a 'retreating forehead.' Many criminals have such foreheads. The Jews are also criminals. Their hair is mostly dark and often curled like the hair of Blacks. Their ears are very big and look like the handle of a coffee cup.

Two other boys add their contribution. One deals with variations, such as blond Jews, and the other with the peculiarities of Jewish movements and speech.

The Jew talks nearly always through his nose.

He often has: A repugnant, foul smell. A fine nose can always smell a Jew.

With these answers, the teacher is satisfied.

He turns the board around. The following verses are written on it and are recited by the children:

From a Jew's face
The wicked Devil speaks to us,
The Devil who, in every country,
Is known as an evil plague.

To be free from the Jew
To again be carefree and happy,
Then must our youth fight with us
To get rid of the Jewish Devil.

CHAPTER THREE

How the Jews Came to Us

"Look at those creatures!" cries Fritz.

"Those sinister Jewish noses! Those lousy beards! Those dirty, sticking-out ears! Those bent legs! Those flat feet! Those stained, fatty clothes! Look how they move their hands about! How they haggle! And those are supposed to be men!"

"And what sort of men?" asks Karl. "They are criminals of the worst sort."

He describes their dealing in various goods, and how, when they have enough money, they get rid of their dirty clothes, cut their beards off, delouse themselves, put on new clothes, and go about as if they were not Jews. In Germany, they speak German and behave as though they were Germans. In France, they speak French and act as Frenchmen. In Italy, they want to be Italians; in Holland, Dutch; in America, Americans; and so on. So they carry on throughout the whole world.

Fritz laughs at this and says, anyhow, they can always be recognized as Jews. Karl nods:

"Naturally, one can spot them if you use your eyes. But unfortunately, there are still many who fall for the Jewish swindle."

THE POISONOUS MUSHROOM

Just look at these guys! The louse-infested beards! The filthy, protruding ears!

THE POISONOUS MUSHROOM

Fritz answers: "Not me! I know the Jews! I also know a verse about them:

> Once they came from the East,
> Dirty, diseased, penniless;
> But in a few years
> They were rich.
>
> Today they dress very well;
> They do not want to be Jews any more.
> So keep your eyes open, and beware:
> Once a Jew, always a Jew!"

THE POISONOUS MUSHROOM

"In the Talmud it is written: Only the Jew is human. Gentile (or non-Jewish) people are not called humans, but animals. Since we Jews see Gentiles as animals, we call them only 'Goy'."

CHAPTER FOUR

What is the Talmud?

Solly is 13 years old. He is the son of the Jew Blumenstock from Langenbach. There is no Jewish school there. Solly therefore has to go to the German school. His schoolmates don't like him. Solly is rude and insolent. There are always fights. And Solly is always responsible for them.

Today Solly doesn't have to go to school. He has to visit a rabbi in the city. A rabbi is a Jewish preacher. And this Jewish preacher wants to see if Solly has diligently studied the teachings of the Jewish religion.

Solly goes to the synagogue. A synagogue is the church of the Jews. The rabbi is waiting for him. He is an old Jew with a long beard and a genuine devil's face. Solly bows. The rabbi leads him to a reading table where there is a large, thick book. It is called the Talmud.

The Talmud is called the secret law-book of the Jews.

The rabbi begins the examination. "Solly, you have a non-Jewish teacher in school. And every day you hear what the Gentiles (the non-Jews) say, what they believe, and the laws by which they live..."

Solly interrupts the rabbi: "Yes, rabbi, I hear that every day. But that doesn't concern me. I am a Jew. I have laws to follow that are entirely different from those of the Gentiles. Our laws are written down in the Talmud."

The rabbi nods. "Right! And now I want to hear what you know about them. Give me a few sayings or proverbs that you have heard in the Gentile school!"

Solly thinks. Then he says: "A proverb of the Gentiles is: Work is no disgrace. What do the Gentiles mean by that?"

"They mean to say that it is no disgrace when one has to work. Do we Jews believe that?"

"No, we don't believe that! In our law book, the Talmud, it is written: *Work is nasty and not to be done.*"

"Therefore we Jews don't work, but mostly engage in business and trading. Gentiles are created to work. In the Talmud it also says: *The rabbi teaches: There is no lower occupation than farming. A Jew should neither plow the field nor plant grain. Commerce is far more bearable than tilling the soil.*"

The rabbi laughs. "You've learned very well. But I know another Talmud passage that you must learn."

He opens the Talmud. Solly reads:

The Gentiles are created to serve the Jews. They must plow, sow, weed, dig, reap, bundle, sift, and grind. The Jews are created to find everything ready for them.

The rabbi continues his examination. "Tell me several more principles or proverbs of the Gentiles!"

Solly answers: "The Gentiles say: *Be ever loyal and upright. Honor is the surest defense.*

What do the Gentiles mean by that?"

"They mean that one should always be honest in life. One should not lie and cheat. That's what the Gentiles say. And what do we Jews do?"

"We may lie and cheat Gentiles. In the Talmud it says:

It is permitted for Jews to cheat Gentiles. All lies are good.

And furthermore, it is written:

It is forbidden for a Jew to cheat his brother. To cheat a Gentile is permitted.

When we loan the Gentiles money, we must demand usurious interest. For in the Talmud it is written:

Concerning robbery, it is taught: Gentiles may not rob each other. The Gentile may not rob the Jews. But the Jews may at any time rob the Gentiles.

It further says:

If a Jew has stolen something from a Gentile and the Gentile discovers it and demands it back, the Jew should simply deny it all. The Jewish court will stand by the Jew."

"It is also permitted for us Jews to buy stolen goods from a thief, when they come from Gentiles.

THE POISONOUS MUSHROOM

We Jews may also sell stolen goods without sinning before our god. Smuggling and tax evasion are also permitted for us Jews. In the Talmud, it is written that we may cheat Gentile authorities of customs and taxes. It says:

Smuggling is permitted, for it is written: You need not pay what you owe.

Also thievery is permitted for Jews. But we may steal only from the Gentiles. The Talmud says:

The words 'You shall not steal' in the Bible refer only to thievery from Jews. Stealing from Gentiles is okay."

"What does that mean?" the rabbi asked.

"That means that we cannot steal from or cheat Jews. But we can cheat Gentiles at any time. That is permitted for us."

The rabbi is satisfied. "Excellent! In conclusion, give me several more laws from the Talmud."

Solly is delighted with the rabbi's praise. Solly says: "In the Talmud it is written: *Only the Jew is human. The Gentile peoples are not called people, rather they are named animals.*

And because we see Gentiles as animals, we call them 'goy.' It is also permitted for us at any time to lie before a Gentile court. In the Talmud it is written:

The Jew is permitted to lie before a Gentile court. Such an oath is always to be seen as compelled. Even when a Jew swears by the name of god, he is allowed to tell a lie, and in his heart to reject the oath he has made.

Furthermore, in the Book of Sirach it says:

Terrify all the nations, O Judah! Lift up your hands against the Gentiles! Incite the wrath of the Gentiles against each other and pour out anger! Shatter the princes who are enemies to the Jews."

Then he says: "You are a fine Talmud student. You will become a real Jew. Always think about what the Talmud demands of you. The teachings and laws of the Talmud are more important and more to be obeyed than the laws of the Old Testament. The teachings of the Talmud are the words of the living Jewish god. He who breaks the laws of the Talmud deserves death. You should think about that throughout your whole life. If you always follow the Talmud laws diligently, you will join our biblical fathers in the Jewish heaven. Amen!"

Murder, thievery, and lies,
Robbery, falsehood, and cheating:
These are all permitted for the Jews,
As every Jewish child knows.

In the Talmud it is written,
What Jews hate and what they love,
What Jews think and how they live,
All is ordained by the Talmud.

THE POISONOUS MUSHROOM

Baptism didn't make a Gentile out of him.

CHAPTER FIVE

WHY THE JEWS LET THEMSELVES BE BAPTIZED

Anne says: "Do you know our Girls' Leader once told us: It is impossible to turn a Black into a German by baptism, and so too, it is impossible to turn a Jew into a non-Jew."

Greta stamps her feet angrily on the ground: "I don't understand these priests who go on baptizing Jews even today. By doing so, they admit a criminal mob into the churches."

Anne concludes: "I believe a time will come when the Christians will curse the clergy who once allowed Jews to enter the Christian Church. For the Jews only want to destroy the Christian Church. And they *will* destroy it, if our clergy go on allowing Jews to enter. There is a saying:

If a Jew comes along
Wanting a priest to baptize him,
Be on your guard and beware:
A Jew always remains a Jew!

Baptismal water helps not a bit.
That does not make the Jew any better!
He is a Devil in time
And he remains so, through eternity!"

THE POISONOUS MUSHROOM

"Daddy, some day when I have my own farm, no Jew will enter my house."

CHAPTER SIX

How a German Peasant was Driven from House and Farm

Little Paul is frightfully shocked. His eyes sparkle with anger. "What a mean Jew!" he says. Then he is silent awhile. Full of loathing, he looks at the Jew. He would love to break the water jug on the Jew's head. But what could he do? That would not help his neighbor.

"Father, when I am grown up and have a farm of my own, I will always think of our neighbor. And no Jew will ever enter my house. I will write on the door: Jews prohibited! And if a Jew were to come in, I would throw him out at once!"

The father nods: "Right, Paul! One should have nothing to do with a Jew. The Jew will always cheat us. The Jew will take from us all we possess. Every peasant must remember that!"

"Yes," says little Paul, "and I will always think of the saying that our teacher has taught us at school:

The peasant prays to the German God:
Oh, keep the hail from us,
Protect us from lightning and flood,
Then we shall have again a good harvest.

THE POISONOUS MUSHROOM

But worse than these plagues,
Never forget, is the Jews!
Be warned: Look out
For the bloodthirsty Jew!"

CHAPTER SEVEN

How Jewish Traders Cheat

It is a festival evening in the village when the Jew turns up with his wares. The Jew flatters the peasant woman and spreads out his wares.

Everything the heart desires, Mr. Levy has for sale. But the German peasant girl turns down his offers.

The Jew persists, and shows her some cloth of the purest wool. "That will make a dress for you, woman, so that you will look like a Baroness or a Princess, like a Queen. And cheap, too, that I can tell you!"

But the peasant woman knows the Jew too well. "I am buying nothing from you," she says, and goes away.

The Jew packs up and goes away cursing. He consoles himself with the knowledge that there are lots of other peasants who can be more easily duped than this one.

Woe to the woman, however, who lets herself be taken in by his chatter. It will happen to her, as has happened to so many other peasant women, once they have let the Jew in. There is no escape. There is an old saying:

THE POISONOUS MUSHROOM

"Farm-woman, have I got something special for you today. Look at this material! You can make a dress from it that will make you look like a baroness, like a countess, like a queen."

THE POISONOUS MUSHROOM

The Jewish hawker
Is a cheat and seducer.
He lies all the time
And you—you pay the price.

So many have gone through the mill.
Would you be saved from these penalties?
Then don't let the Jew come in
And buy only from a German!

THE POISONOUS MUSHROOM

"Here, kids, I have some candy for you. But you both have to come with me."

CHAPTER EIGHT

The Experience of Hans and Else with a Strange Man

Else suddenly has plenty of candies. Hans asks where they came from.

"I got them from a strange man," she says. "But don't tell mother! The man strictly forbids me to do so!" Hans is curious. They arrange to go see him together. The man wants them to go with him.

But Hans hesitates—he thinks: "What does the man want of us? Why should we go with him?"

Suddenly a great fear comes over him.

"You are a Jew!" he cries, and, seizing his sister, runs off as fast as his legs will carry him.

At the corner of the street he meets a policeman. Quickly, Hans tells his story. The policeman gets on his motorbike and soon captures the strange man. He handcuffs him and takes him to prison.

At home, afterward, there is great rejoicing. The police praise Hans for being a brave lad. His mother gives him a large piece of chocolate while teaching him the following saying:

THE POISONOUS MUSHROOM

A devil goes through the land,
He is the Jew, known to us all
As murderer of the people and polluter of the races,
The terror of children in every country!

He wants to ruin the youth.
He wants all people to perish.
Have nothing to do with a Jew.
Then you'll be happy and carefree!

CHAPTER NINE

INGE'S VISIT TO A JEWISH DOCTOR

Inge is sick. For several days she has had a light fever and a headache. But Inge did not want to go to the doctor.

"Why go to the doctor for such a small thing?" she said again and again when her mother suggested it. Finally her mother insisted.

"March! Go to Doctor Bernstein and let him examine you!" her mother ordered.

"Why Doctor Bernstein? He's a Jew! And no real German girl goes to a Jew," Inge replied.

Her mother laughed. "Don't talk nonsense! Jewish doctors are all right. Others are always chattering nonsense about it at your League of German Girls meetings. What do those girls know about it?"

Inge protested. "Mother, you can say what you want, but you can't attack the League of German Girls. You should know that we German Girls understand the Jewish Question better than many of our parents. Our Girls' Leader gives a short talk about the Jews nearly every week. Just recently she said: 'A German should not go to a Jewish doctor! Particularly not a German girl! Because the Jews

THE POISONOUS MUSHROOM

Two criminal eyes flashed behind the glasses, and the fat lips grinned.

want to destroy the German people. Many girls who went to a Jewish doctor for healing found sickness and shame instead!' That's what our Girls' Leader said, Mother. And she's right!"

Her mother grew impatient. "You always think you know more than the grown-ups. What you said just isn't true. Look, Inge. I know Doctor Bernstein well. He is a fine doctor."

"But he's a Jew! And the Jews are our deadly enemies," Inge replied.

Now her mother became really angry. "That's enough, you naughty child! Go to Doctor Bernstein right now! If you don't, I'll teach you how to obey me!" Her mother yelled and raised her hand.

Inge did not want to be disobedient, so she went—to the Jewish doctor Bernstein!

Inge sits in the waiting room of the Jewish doctor. She has to wait a long time. She looks through the magazines that are on the table. But she is much too nervous to be able to read more than a few sentences. Again and again, she thinks back on the conversation with her mother. And again and again, she recalls the warning of her Girls' Leader: 'A German must not go to a Jewish doctor! Particularly a German girl! Many girls who went to a Jewish doctor for healing found sickness and shame instead!'

As Inge entered the waiting room, she had a strange experience. From the doctor's examination room, she heard someone crying. She heard a girl's voice: "Doctor! Doctor! Leave me alone!"

THE POISONOUS MUSHROOM

Then she heard a man's scornful laugh. Then all was suddenly silent. Breathlessly, Inge listened.

"What does all that mean?" she asked herself, and her heart beat faster. Once again, she thought of the warnings of her League of German Girls' Leader.

Inge has been waiting for an hour. Again she picks up the magazines and tries to read. Then the door opens. Inge looks up. The Jew appears. A cry comes from Inge's mouth. Terrified, she lets the newspaper drop. Terrified, she jumps up. Her eyes stare into the face of the Jewish doctor.

And this face is the face of the Devil. In the middle of this devilish face sits an enormous crooked nose. Behind the glasses glare two criminal eyes. And a grin runs across the protruding lips. A grin that wants to say: 'Now I have you at last, little German girl!'

The Jew comes toward her. His fat fingers grasp for her. But now Inge has recovered. Before the Jew can grab her, she slaps his fat face. Then a leap to the door. Breathlessly Inge runs down the steps. Breathlessly she dashes out of the Jew's office.

In tears, she returns home. Her mother is shocked to see her child. "For God's sake, Inge! What happened?"

It's a long time before the child can say anything. Finally, Inge tells about her experience with the Jew doctor. Her mother listens in horror. And when Inge finishes her story, her mother lowers her head in shame.

"Inge, I shouldn't have sent you to a Jewish doctor. When you left, I regretted it. I couldn't relax. I wanted to call you back. I suddenly suspected that you were right. I suspected that something would happen to you. But everything came out all right, thank God!" Her mother moans, and tries to conceal her tears.

Gradually Inge calms down. She laughs again. "Mother, you've done a lot for me. Thank you. But you have to promise me something: about the League of German Girls…"

Her mother doesn't let her finish. "I know what you want to say, Inge. I promise. I'm finding that one can learn even from you children."

Inge nods. "You're right, Mother. We German Girls, we know what we want, even if we are not always understood. Mother, you taught me many sayings. Today I want to give you one to learn." And slowly and wisely, Inge says:

> "The Devil, it was he
> Who sent the Jew doctor to Germany.
> Like a devil, he contaminates
> The German woman, Germany's honor.
>
> The German people, they'll not be sound
> Unless very soon, a way is found
> To German healing, German ways,
> To German doctors in future days.

THE POISONOUS MUSHROOM

A man was waiting for me at the station. He tipped his hat and was very friendly to me. But I could tell immediately that he was a Jew.

CHAPTER TEN

HOW THE JEW TREATS HIS DOMESTIC HELP

This story tells of a 23-year-old Rosa, who sought a job in house-cleaning, using a Jewish agency in Vienna. For four weeks, her parents heard nothing from her. They are troubled. Finally a letter comes from Rosa, telling how she was trafficked and her experiences, and how, finally, she reached a Jewish home in England, via the Jewish Agency.

In England: "They were again Jews. I got only small wages and had to work from early morning till late at night. I had almost nothing to eat. The Jews treated me as if I were a dog. I was constantly insulted."

The letter goes on to tell how she was rescued by the wife of a good German businessman, who was on a visit to London. "They rescued me from slavery. They even bought me a return ticket."

Rosa concludes: "The Jew is a devil. I shall hate him as long as I live. And I shall always think of the saying I heard yesterday:

THE POISONOUS MUSHROOM

German woman, great or small,
The Jew calls you simply: Goyim.
He hates you, corrupts you,
Treats you worse than cattle.

If a girl wants to keep herself pure
Let her steer clear of the Jews!
If she wants to make good in life's struggle,
Let her have nothing to do with the Jews!"

CHAPTER ELEVEN

HOW TWO WOMEN WERE TRICKED BY JEWISH LAWYERS

This story tells how a Jewish lawyer, by making the same promises to two German women, complainant and defendant, takes fees from both. In the court, judgment is given: Both women are guilty. Both must pay.

After the court proceedings, the two Jewish lawyers who have so arranged the case congratulate one another on the good business they have done: "Now we have jewed the two Goys of their money, we can put it in our sack!"

The two German women recognize they have been cheated, make peace with one another, and take the experience as a warning never to quarrel again, and: "Never to go again to Jewish lawyers. We will remember all our lives this saying:

THE POISONOUS MUSHROOM

"Well, Mr. Morgenthau, we did a good piece of business today." "Splendid, Mr. Silberstein. We took the lovely money from the two Goy women and can put it in our own pockets."

THE POISONOUS MUSHROOM

The Jewish lawyer
Has no feeling for justice.
He only goes to court
Because of the money.

Whether brave and good people
Wear themselves out and bleed,
Leaves the Jew completely cold.
Never go to a Jewish lawyer!"

THE POISONOUS MUSHROOM

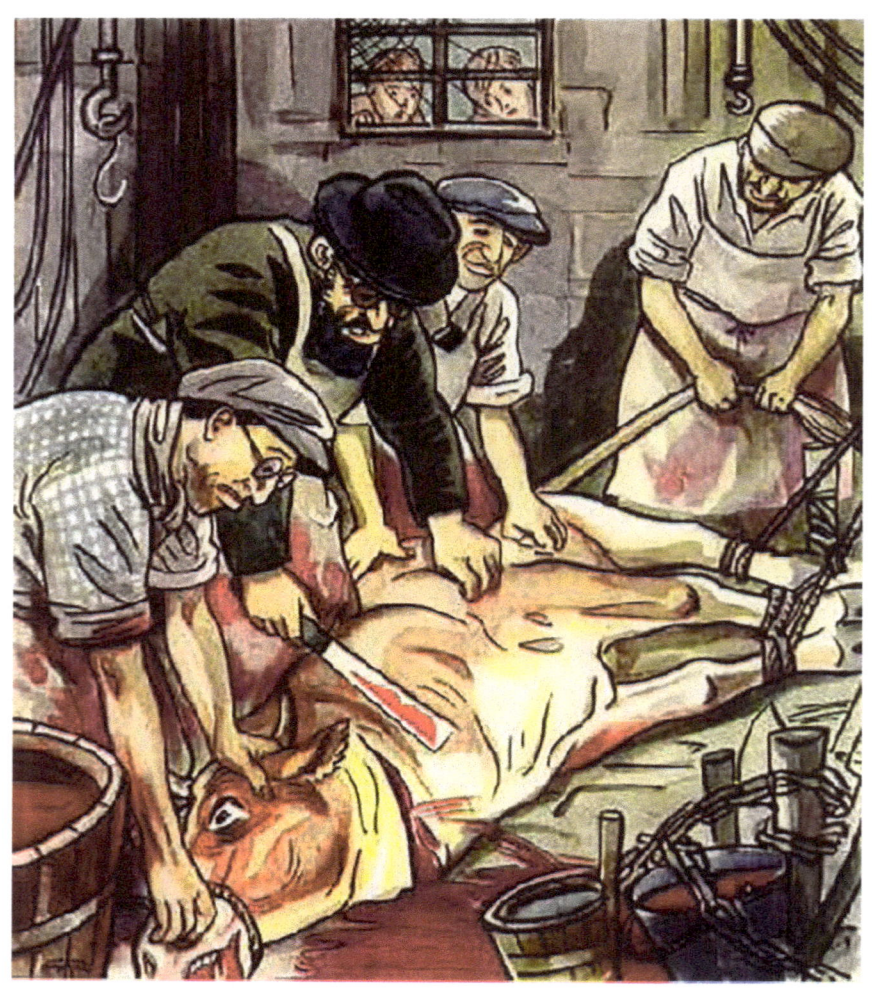

The animal fell once more to the ground. Slowly it died. The Jews stood around and laughed.

CHAPTER TWELVE

HOW JEWS TORMENT ANIMALS

In this story, two boys, Kurt and Otto, go to a Jewish slaughterhouse and hide themselves where they can watch the Jews killing a cow. The process of holding the cow and the operation are described, involving callous brutality and gloating on the part of the Jewish butchers. Four Jews hold down the cow while its neck is being cut.

The Jews stand there and—laugh. At the end, Otto says: "Kurt, now I believe you. The Jews are the meanest people in the world."

Kurt answers: "Yes, the Jews are a murderous people. With the same brutality and lust for blood with which they kill animals, they also kill human beings. Have you ever heard of ritual murders? On such occasions, the Jews kill boys and girls, men and women. From the earliest days, Jews have been murderers. They are Devils in human form. There is a saying:

THE POISONOUS MUSHROOM

Anger, envy, hatred, rage,
Are in the blood of the Jew,
Towards every people on the Earth
Who do not belong to the Chosen.

He kills animals and men,
His bloodlust knows no bounds.
The world can only recover
When it is rid of the Jew."

CHAPTER THIRTEEN

WHAT JESUS SAID ABOUT THE JEWS

A peasant mother returning from work in the fields, with her three children, pauses in front of a cross with Jesus Christ. The mother talks to them about the wickedness of the Jews.

She points to the cross, which stands by the road: "Children, look there! The man who hangs on the cross was one of the greatest enemies of the Jews of all time. He knew the Jews in all their corruption and meanness. Once he drove the Jews out with a whip, because they were carrying on their money-dealings in the church. He called the Jews: Killers of men from the beginning. By that he meant that the Jews, in all times, have been murderers."

"He further said to the Jews: 'Your father is the Devil!' Do you know, children, what that means? It means that the Jews descend from the Devil. And because they descend from the Devil, they can only live like devils. So they commit one crime after another."

The children look thoughtfully at the cross.

Mother continues: "Because this man knew the Jews, because he proclaimed the truth to the world,

THE POISONOUS MUSHROOM

When you see a cross, remember the gruesome act of murder committed by the Jews on Golgotha.

he had to die. Hence the Jews murdered him. They drove nails through his hands and feet and let him slowly bleed. In such a horrible way, the Jews took their revenge. And in a similar way, they have killed many others who had the courage to tell the truth about the Jews."

"Always remember these things, children. When you see the cross, think of the terrible murder by the Jews on Golgotha. Remember that the Jews are children of the Devil and human murderers. Remember the saying:

> As long as Jews have been on Earth
> There have been enemies of the Jews.
> They gave warning of the Jewish blood
> And even sacrificed their own blood,
>
> So that the world might know the Devil
> And not plunge into ruin;
> So that the world might soon be freed
> From its slavery to the Jew."

THE POISONOUS MUSHROOM

The god of the Jews is money. To earn money, he commits the greatest crimes. He will not rest until he can sit on a huge money sack, until he has become the Money King.

CHAPTER FOURTEEN

MONEY IS THE GOD OF THE JEWS

Liselotte looks out the cottage window towards evening and talks to her mother about the hard way in which father has to work. She says: "Do you know, Mother, what I sometimes wish? I would like to be rich. Very rich! And with my money, I would make people happy. I would love to help the poor!"

They go on talking. Liselotte asks: "Tell me, Mother, how does it happen that the Jews are so rich? Our teacher has told us at school that there are thousands of Jews in the world who are millionaires. And yet the Jews do not work. It is the non-Jews who must work. The Jew only trades. But one cannot become a millionaire by trading with paper, bones, old clothing, and furniture!"

Mother explains how it is done. "The Jew doesn't care when the cheated non-Jew goes hungry. Jews have no pity. They strive for one thing: money. They don't give two hoots how they get it."

Liselotte asks how they can behave in this mean way. Mother answers: "Child, one thing you must realize. The Jew is not a person like us. The Jew is a Devil. And a Devil has no sense of honor. A Devil deals only in meanness and crime."

"You have read your Bible, Liselotte. There it says the Jewish god once said to the Jews: 'You must eat up the people of the earth!' Do you know what that means? It means the Jew should destroy all other peoples. They should bleed and exploit them till they die. That is what it means."

Liselotte tries to understand these things.

Mother continues: "Yes, my child, that's the Jew! The god of the Jews is gold. There is no crime he would not commit to get it. He has no rest till he can sit on the top of a gold sack. He has no rest till he has become Money King. And with this money, he would make us all into slaves and destroy us. With this money, he seeks to dominate the whole world. All this is contained in this saying:

> The Jew has only one idea in this world:
> It is: Money, Money, Money!
> By every kind of trick and deceit
> To make himself immeasurably rich.
>
> What does he care for scorn and contempt!
> Money was and is his god!
> Through money, he hopes to rule over us,
> And achieve mastery of the world.

CHAPTER FIFTEEN

How Mr. Hartmann became a National Socialist

This story tells how a decent German worker, after listening to the talk of a Jewish speaker in a communist meeting, turns away in disgust and joins the National Socialists of Herr Hitler.

The Hitler Youth group is out for a hike. On the way, they meet Mr. Hartmann and they invite him to tell them a story. Mr. Hartmann tells how, years ago, unemployed, he became a communist. He describes the communist meetings.

One day he observed that the leaders were Jews: "And as one of the Jews was always talking about Russia and always saying it was best there, I grew angry and interrupted: 'Why are you always talking about Russia? We are German workers! Yes, we're Germans. We want to hear something about Germany, not Russia!'"

He goes on to tell how the speaker grew fearfully angry and finally called out: "What do we care about Germany? All that matters is that we get by and have a good time!"

THE POISONOUS MUSHROOM

The Jew cries: "We don't care about Germany. The main thing is that things go well for us."

THE POISONOUS MUSHROOM

"Now I knew enough. We workers would become traitors to the nation. We would cooperate with the Jews for the ruin of Germany. I would not be a traitor to the Fatherland. No, never! I turned my back on the Jews and left the meeting. Three others came with me. That night I could not sleep. But then I knew what to do. I left the communist party."

"Later, I found my way to Adolf Hitler. And I say to you: I will stay with Hitler as long as I live. I knew the Jews. I will always think of the song that we workers sang:

> If a people wants to be powerful
> It must hold firmly together.
> Strikes and walkouts and a class struggle
> Are the ruin of a nation.
>
> This the world has been taught often enough
> Throughout the centuries.
> Eternal peace will only come
> When we have been freed from the Jews."

THE POISONOUS MUSHROOM

"People are always saying that we Jews cheat other people, that we lie and deceive. Not a word of it is true. We Jews are the most decent people in the world."

CHAPTER SIXTEEN

ARE THERE DECENT JEWS?

Four Germans sit talking in a cafe. One is a Jew, Salomon, who is telling the others that the Jews are the most decent people to be found anywhere.

Zimmermann won't have it, and cites cases of Jewish rogues he has met. The Jew gets uneasy, and seeks a way out by saying: "Oh well, but those are exceptions!" A peasant joins in the talk and supports Zimmermann.

Salomon gets angry. He has paid for the beer and still must listen to that sort of talk from them.

"You talk a lot of stupid nonsense!" he cries, "but not a word about decent Jews. And there are plenty of decent Jews. Am I not one? Was I not a soldier at the Front? Did I not defend the Fatherland? Have I not paid for your beer, you impudent creatures, you stupid Goys!"

There is silence in the room.

Then a worker gets up who has said little, and throws a coin to the Jew. "You are finished, Salomon. Here's your money. We will not have you paying for us. But now you shall have the truth! You liar! You never heard a bullet. You were indispensable, and stayed at home profiteering, then you were with the Reds, yelling 'Down with Germany! Long live the World Revolution!' And now you are a decent Jew? Not a bit of it! There aren't any decent Jews."

Salomon picks up his hat and runs like the Devil from the cafe. Everybody laughs.

"What a pity he has gone!" says Zimmermann. "I would like to have repeated the following saying to him:

> So often we hear the tale
> How brave such-and-such a Jew was.
> How he gave his money to the poor
> And was an angel in the world.
>
> A Jew, like a pure angel?
> That must be a fairy tale!
> Who invents such things?
> It's the Jew, himself, who does it!"

CHAPTER SEVENTEEN

No Salvation Without Solving the Jewish Question

The members of the Hitler Boys' Club are proud of their black uniform. "We are the real Hitler men," they say. Although 'men' is a bit overdone, they are right in one thing: the boys are loyal to the Führer in life and death.

The boys are talking—in this concluding story—among themselves. One of them describes a National Socialist Party march in Munich on the previous November 9th:

"Next to the Führer was General Göring, who was formerly severely wounded at the Feldherrnhalle. I saw, too, Reich Ministers Doctor Goebbels, Frick, Rust, and the Reich Leader Rosenberg, Amann, Schwarz, our Reich Youth Leader Schirach, and many other old campaigners. In front of the Führer, they carried the Swastika Flag, which received its consecration on November 9th, 1923. And in front of the Swastika Flag marched a man who, in 1923, was also in the front of the battle: Julius Streicher."

Another boy says: "We know him all right. He is the enemy of the Jews. That's why all the Jews hate him."

THE POISONOUS MUSHROOM

"He who fights the Jews battles the Devil." — *Julius Streicher.*

THE POISONOUS MUSHROOM

"You are right," says another. "The Jews hate and insult only those whom they most fear. And they are afraid of Streicher."

Another boy, hitherto silent, draws attention to a poster, which reads: "Julius Streicher is speaking in the People's Hall on 'The Jews are our Misfortune!'"

"Let's go," says Konrad. "I've long wanted to hear him."

Erich says: "I heard him once in a meeting two years ago." "Tell us about him!" cry the other two boys.

Erich explains: "The meeting was packed. Thousands of people were there. At first, Streicher spoke about the years of struggle and the great achievements of the Hitler Reich. Then he came to the Jewish Question. What he said was so clear and simple that even we youngsters could understand. He took his examples always from life itself. Once he was very funny and made jokes, so we all had to laugh. Then he became deeply earnest and it was so still in the room, you could have heard a pin drop. He spoke of the Jews and their revolting crimes. He spoke of the great danger the Jews were to the whole world: Without a solution to the Jewish Question, there is no salvation for mankind!"

"That's what he said to us. We all understood. And when, at the end, he had called *'Sieg Heil!'* for the Führer, we had a storm of enthusiasm for him. Streicher had spoken for two hours, but it only seemed like a few minutes to us."

"Yes, my dear friends! I will always think of that meeting. And I will never forget the chorus which we heard at the end of the gathering:

'From Hitler's Germany resounds a cry to the whole world: Free yourselves from the Jewish hand, and save both people and Fatherland!'"

> The world awakes in Judah's chains;
> Germany alone it knows can save!
>
> Through German ideas and German being
> The whole world will one day be restored.

www.ingramcontent.com/pod-product-compliance
Lightning Source LLC
Chambersburg PA
CBHW061225070526
44584CB00029B/3984